"But who made God?"

Marieke Anschütz

"But who made God?"

Religion and
your growing child

Floris Books

Translated by Polly Lawson

First published in Dutch under the title
Over religieuze opvoeding
by Uitgeverij Christofoor, Zeist, 1988.

First published in English by Floris Books in 1991.

British Library CIP available

ISBN 0–86315–136–1

Printed in Great Britain
by Billing & Sons Ltd, Worcester

Contents

A word in advance

When we are dealing with children, we are working in and with a naturally religious element. Characteristic of young children is the way in which they accept the lead of the grown-up, the limitless trust with which they come to us, and the openness with which they take in the marvels of the world. Acceptance, limitless trust and openness: these characteristics are also those of true religion, and so we may well speak of the "naturally religious" nature of the child.

In order to practise a trade or profession, we undergo training and acquire skills. In religion, though, acquired skills and confidence in our abilities are far less important than the fact that we are willing. Performance in a trade, profession or calling is determined mostly by ability. But in religion, our performance is determined not by our ability but by our will.

Religion is not just one isolated component or subdivision of education; it permeates all our activity with children, both in a positive and a negative sense. Every education should really be religious in nature, for religiousness is not confined to any one religious denomination. It is a way of being, a way of acting out of a more or less conscious knowledge of what the Gospels teach about the life, death and resurrection of one who is called among other things "the Lord of Destiny."

A certain fundamental attitude is essential for religiousness in education, namely an unconditional readiness to serve. Anyone who feels inadequate in this respect has only to bear in mind the delightfully fresh and original thought that "no pencil is so ordinary that a Michelangelo could not create a masterpiece with it."

But let us go back to the characteristics of the young child, those characteristics which are also those of the religious element: acceptance, unlimited trust and openness. What is acceptance other than a feeling of being cared for and protected in the hand of God whatever destiny may bring? Acceptance gives us inner certainty and calm. It is what we mean by the rather time–worn word "faith." What is unlimited trust other than keeping the true being of the other person in view through all the shadowy aspects of personality? Using an even more overworked word we can call this "love." And what is openness other than unprejudiced hope in what is striving to come into being, however faulty its nature? In his first letter to the Corinthians, the Apostle Paul names these three, and his words are as true as ever: "So faith, hope, love abide, these three: but the greatest of these is love." (1 Cor.13:13)

Children watch us, they see us in what we do, in what we say, indeed in what we think, and that means that we must live out our religion in front of them. That is not easy, but we can strive to do so with a cool head and a warm heart. This book is intended as a help in this direction.

— 1 —

Travelling with ourselves

The main precondition for anyone who would give something is that they should first have something to give. We cannot foster the natural religiousness of a child unless we carry a religious element in ourselves. What the child possesses unconsciously and by nature, has to be regained by us through thought. We cannot bring up children by instinct. We must seek ways of arriving at a conscious knowledge of what used to be known instinctively, for the new connection to the spiritual world is to be made by way of thought.

My mother always said: "I did not bring you children up; you brought *me* up." An unusual but deeply wise observation for a woman who had herself grown up in times of peace and security, but who brought up her own children in a time of world war when people did not stay in any one place for long and there was no sense in growing attached to a particular house and home, for everything might be lost from one day to the next. Then it was a question of settling down again in a new place, establishing new habits and patterns of life. For those who lived through such times, this insecurity has remained, and the mood of the old settled times will never return. But something else has taken its place: we have learnt a lesson. We have learned to live adaptably, we have learnt constantly to acquire new norms and values. We have learnt to direct our attachments no longer exclusively to worldly goods and to earthly security. It is a lesson which we have to wrestle with daily, for to acquire this kind of inner security requires a whole lifetime; indeed it is questionable whether even one lifetime is sufficient.

Too great adaptability however can have a negative effect. The evil of these times is that we have forgotten how to make true connections. There is often so much rush that there is not enough time to give our attention to anything else but ourselves and our own concerns. In these times we are so used to rapid changes that we do not have the peace in which to grow attached to anything or anyone. Older attachments are broken off leaving us with a sense of insecurity.

The first thing in our self-education is to have *patience with ourselves*. The birth of a child can make us want to do lots of things: we want to start with all sorts of things simultaneously, so that much is begun but nothing carried through. Therefore we must be strict with ourselves. Everything which we would make our own, needs time to grow. Our spiritual food must be digested. Watch how that happens with chil-

12

dren. When we play a game with a toddler, recite a nursery rhyme or an "action rhyme" or tell a story, we hear children say: "Do it again!" They keep on asking for the words and actions to be repeated until these are absorbed right into their being and united with their physical body.

Whereas the child acquires capabilities and attributes by unconscious and natural repetition, we adults have to make a conscious effort in the performance of our exercises. We must persevere until we notice that the repetition does us good and we notice that something comes "from beyond" which helps us and we find ourselves borne along by a stream. Even so we must not forget that we ourselves must swim and keep our heads above water.

Wonder is the beginning of all wisdom. Why do we do certain things, and especially why do we *not* do certain things? In these turbulent times it is not easy to be a "mother" in the fullest sense of the word: meaning warmth, protection, life, the foundation of our existence. "Motherhood" appears to be such a distant and unattainable ideal, there is so much else that is thrust upon us which we would gladly push aside but which we must deal with. We see that things around us are not as they were: the norms have altered, customs have changed, old usages have disappeared. The carrying power of a religious community for many people has been lost. Thus it is as if inwardly we are more impoverished. It is clear that things are no longer "handed to us on a plate." We ourselves have to buckle to and practise becoming conscious till it tingles in our finger-tips. What for instance does it mean when we say: "Religious upbringing has to start with the world which the child experiences"? That world is really much greater and wider than we normally realize. As adults we are so accustomed to the thought that we can do everything and that the child still has to learn. It is true that we can instruct the child in worldly things, but once we start to perceive the child's true nature then we realize that the child can instruct us in heavenly matters. There are three things which we then notice in children: their uninhibited attitude to us, the intensity with which they unite with things and the sunny trust which they give us. These three are the principal qualities of religiousness.

Are we able to retain anything from our own childhood days? What can the child learn from us that is important? Goethe gives an answer in his *Wilhelm Meister:* "In reality we do not need to educate, we must only take care that the natural disposition of the person can develop. There is however only one thing which really makes the human being a human being, but which does not develop by itself, but which we can only learn from and through other people, and that is reverence."

This then is the *second* thing which we, whether we possess much or little knowledge, must make the basis of our self-education: the development of respect and reverence in ourselves.

What is reverence? It is to allow things and people to stand in their own worth. It is also to look at things differently, so that we see more than the earthly reality. It is the awakening of an organ of perception by which we learn a kind of listening. We learn to listen to what lies behind things; behind children's questions, for instance. What are the children actually asking? One evening, looking back on the day, a little girl asks: "Is it the same for everyone, even for Granny, when you say Thursday?" If our deeper perception is not working properly, we will give an ordinary answer, smiling indulgently at the silly question; but if we are truly listening within us, we can hear the enormous space behind this question, a space which encompasses the whole of mankind and history. Then we are struck by the tremendous implications of a simple but unusual question and we feel as if we are standing dizzily at the edge of a precipice, and an intense feeling of gratitude comes over us that we have been able to hear.

Reverence is something which we can practise daily wherever we are and it becomes easier when we know that it has to do with attentiveness. Those who are looking after children at home can find objects in their surroundings to ponder on with wonder and gratitude: ordinary things such as clean washing that smells so nice, the motes dancing in the sunbeams, the water running out of the bath making such a funny gurgling as it swirls round the plughole, the onion that wears so many petticoats, or our breath with which we cool the hot tea but with which we warm our hands in winter. Those who work away from home can try to keep aside a few moments each day to look with real attention at the world around us, even little things that may strike us while waiting for the tram or bus: the seasonal change of an isolated tree in the town land-scape; or just the sun catching the houses opposite.

Schools do not teach upbringing. Life itself must be our school: we learn mostly as we work at it. But it is good if we can do more. By talking and listening to others we can discover guidelines for our actions, and in books we can find detailed information and advice on more complicated problems, such as children's illnesses. What, for instance, are we do we do about immunization? What do we do when a child is ill? If we learn to recognize the symptoms, we do not need to get into a panic. Our calm assurance radiates out over the sick child and helps the child to become healthy again.

Thus the development of "consciousness" or of "being conscious" is the *third* element to which we direct our endeavours in self-education. Here belongs, too, the need to acquire deeper insight into the development of a child. Often we have neither the time nor the inclination to read much. However, if we are in a position to observe young children around us every day we can often experience amusing situations, little squabbles, funny or striking utterances. We resolve to note them down but we always seem to forget them sooner than we thought. So it is a good idea to have paper and pencil handy to write down what the little ones say, especially when they are learning to talk. What words of the evening prayer or grace at table are first spoken? How does the child set about building with blocks? Do other children do it differently? How do they learn to walk? What is the dominant characteristic of each child? By making notes in this simple way, each of us can acquire insights into the development of the child who is entrusted to us.

A help in upbringing which is to be warmly recommended is to reflect consciously on the child. Before we go to sleep we should call the child to mind and try to see the whole person as objectively as possible. It is very important how we regard a child: whether with pride, annoyance, respect, admiration or in whatever other manner; or whether we withhold our own feelings and try to see objectively the difficulties which we have with the child or the behaviour which we find annoying. Why does this particular child make things so difficult for himself and others? What is he going to do with his life here on earth? Should we have more trust in those qualities which we glimpse but cannot yet perceive fully? Looking in this way makes it possible for us to see a person differently. It is the light of selflessness, of humility, of love and it enables us truly to look at the child with "different eyes." We come to see that this approach works and that a situation which had become rigid can now be made fluid again. We discover an opening and a possibility of going further. Thus upbringing, and certainly the morality of it, must always be closely connected with self–education. When we overcome something in ourselves this influences the child. "Up to the fourteenth year the child lives in the thought–life of its mother," I once heard an old experienced teacher say. I think that we must add: "and in the inner life of all those who are closely connected with the growing child."

The *fourth* element of self-education is the practice of reviewing the day. To look back at what lies behind us, beginning with the present, was often recommended by Rudolf Steiner as a good exercise in order to get a grip on our own actions and what we leave undone. Working backwards from evening to morning, we recall the events of the day, stopping longer at special events. Thus we learn to look with a certain objectivity at what we have done, felt and thought. Finally the transition from day to night is best travelled if we let our last thoughts rest on the world towards which our being is bound.

The moments before we go to sleep are precious, but equally valuable are those of the early morning, for immediately after waking there is a chance to create a soul-space for ourselves. Once we are up, before we know it we are halfway through the morning. Then we have the unsatisfactory feeling that we have not quite "come to." This brings us to the *fifth* element of self-education, which is indeed the most essential: to create for ourselves our own space in the day. It may be possible somewhere in between other things to "take a breather," but many have found it good to get up very early while the house is still quiet and the early-

morning sound of the birds outside can still be heard.
We can briefly dwell on a beautiful poem, a part of
the Gospels with a particular theme, a prayer or verse.
Here, too, the most important thing is that we raise our
thoughts above earthly existence, so that strength may
be given to us to do our daily work.

Through working at ourselves, we can maintain the
fire that infuses us in good moments. The "free time"
which we make for ourselves is not a luxury, nor is it
a waste of time but works on through the whole day.
The housework, looking after the family, outside tasks
which we have taken on — all these things become
easier when we know ourselves strengthened by a
power which we have called forth through our own
efforts. The inner calm and clarity which we acquire,
make clear more than anything else that self–education
is an indispensable part of the child's upbringing. *Ora
et Labora* is the ancient motto of an order of monks
and nuns. Pray and work, not the other way round.
Prayer, sincere and selfless, in whatever form, always
means seeking union with the spiritual world. Prayer
makes our work fruitful in this world so that we can
pursue our tasks with true enthusiasm (from the Greek
en–theos meaning "in God").

— 2 —

The first year

We are born into the physical world through the doorway of our mother, and I address myself here to those who are mothers.

As a mother, during the birth of a child and for some weeks after, you feel yourself living in a borderland between heaven and Earth. There is an openness upwards to everything that weaves invisibly round the new little human child — an openness that makes you vulnerable to strong impressions. Pregnancy, forty weeks long, is not only a time of preparation for the growing child, it is just as much a time of preparing for the mother-to-be. Not only do you become physically so changed that you can hardly recognize yourself, but you notice also that you are changing inwardly. Just as everything in your body is directing itself towards the birth so everything in your mind revolves round the coming child. This concentration of forces in the mother has the effect of shutting her off from the outside world. Not only does the physical body change but an inner world grows and becomes perceptible, opening up towards the spiritual world. It is an openness which at other times is much harder to attain.

In the forty days after childbirth you gradually grow stronger, not so vulnerable. You don't burst into tears so easily, you have taken on looking after the house and home again, and your care of the newly born child is becoming much easier. In a word, the lying-in time is over. But at the same time something else has come to an end: the doorway to the spiritual world where you were able to stand in that first glowing period, warm and rosy, open to lovely thoughts and good wishes. That door is shut but the key is put in your hand: namely the child whom you carried beneath your heart.

There is someone for whom this applies perhaps even more strongly than for the mother and that is the father. He cannot be the physical doorway into the world for his child, but inwardly he can enact the process of birth, and then he will notice, often to his own surprise, that a wonderful warmth comes into his voice, a new tenderness in his actions, and a quiet reverence in his gaze. The father stands behind the mother looking over her shoulder with her into the future, to all that is trying to come into being. For him, too, the child can be a key to the Kingdom of God.

——— o Θ o ———

Our life stretches between birth and death. The hour of death lies in the future. We know for a certainty that death will come to us although we do not know the exact moment. Nor can we remember anything about the moment of our birth. All we know for sure is that it once was. It is in the present that we live.

Until the child is born, it lies enveloped in its mother's womb. Normally it is the head which is born first: this is the "oldest" part of the body and the most formed. Body and limbs slide out gently after. All is soft and round in the new-born child, small and vulnerable. At each new birth, there is a sense of wonder that everything seems to be there just right, not too much and not too little. The pre-natal roundness remains visible for a long time, arms and legs are drawn up and constantly in motion. It takes a whole year for the round form to stretch out fully.

The new-born baby's eyes are dark and as if turned in upon themselves. Hidden deep behind the earnest eyes lies the riddle of the child's personality. The question comes into our mind: "Who are you?" "What are you going to do on earth?" In perfect trust and acceptance the child comes into the world and makes a direct claim upon us. It requires our help for many years in order to find its way on earth.

When the child is born, the circuit of its own blood becomes closed. The connection with the mother is cut off. The first cry has started his breathing — physi-cally the child is now an independent being in a "home" which stands on its own, an individual, an undivided creature. Thus from birth to death, the individual stands apart.

Just as a plant sprouts and sends forth one leaf after another under the influence of light and air, of water and warmth, so the young child brings forth abilities and lets them shine in the warmth of our devotion. The developmental process starts at the head and works downwards. During the first weeks the child sleeps a lot, but it is nonetheless the eyes that are the first to awaken to the world. They soon "fasten" on to the little bell above the cot and bring the head to rest. After a time the hands follow, trying to get hold of the little toy while the baby's body stretches. Much later it is the feet which seek security on the ground in order to carry the whole little person. Those constant agitated movements which remind us of water slowly disappear.

The first year of life is full of moments of celebration, as every newly acquired skill or development — the first smile, for instance — is greeted with joy. Following the deeply felt pregnancy and birth itself, as a kind of compensation there comes the first remarkable smile with its mystery, as if all at once the deeply hidden kernel, something of the uniqueness of the child, comes to the surface. It is as if the child recognizes something, and rediscovers in the loving look of the mother and father something already known from before birth. That first smile of recognition brings joy, with the first real meeting, person to person, taking place in the moment when eye gazes into eye.

Around the fifth month we notice that the baby, lying down, tries to roll in a particular direction. With all the effort put into it, there is much grunting and groaning. We feel the urge to help, but it is better if we do not help. In the same way it is better not to put into the child's hand straight away the ball which it is reaching for. If we resist the temptation to interfere, and we restrain ourselves we may see something extraordinarily exciting; we are granted a glimpse into the workshop of tremendous forces, forces of growth forming the child. These are really divine forces which are operating, to be watched only with due reverence.

At the end of the first year "the highest point" is reached: the child begins "to stand on his own feet." The feet are still as round as little cushions but the human stance is recognizable: standing in a vertical line, against gravity, with the hands free to work in the world. The most important events in life can often happen at an unexpected moment; look at death, for instance. Equally unexpected is the moment in life when we first stand upright. For some time the signs were there that the great day was approaching; but then just at the vital moment our attention was on something else and at that very moment it happened. There are rare moments like this in our lives, moments with a quality and depth which the eye alone cannot really observe, and which no clicking camera will ever capture.

A little boy was scrabbling round the room. Sometimes he pulled himself up by a chair or he took a few steps beside the bench. The little feet stood on the ground more and more firmly but as yet there was no sign of him standing on his own. It looked as if he was waiting for something. Then it happened. Mother was busy in the kitchen and heard the child calling. When she came into the room her heart gave a leap. Her little son was right in the middle of the floor far from any support. He was calling: "Up, up, up!" and with each "up" he reached up like an athlete does, from his knees. The mother had the impression that the child was being drawn up till he stood in free space. What struck her most was the beaming smile on the child's face as he took three resolute steps and then collapsed back into a crouching position.

For three weeks after that, the child "forgot" how to walk until one day the mother left the house to go shopping. An older girl who was living with the family at that time was in the room practising her 'cello. She was so deep in her practice that she only noticed when the little boy was right beside her. The room filled with wonderful sounds and the child was affected and uplifted by it. He had discovered the source of that remarkable sound, stood up as if enchanted and walked straight to that powerfully vibrating instrument. From that moment on, he walked, and never "forgot" again.

3

Developing language

The toddler beside me is walking on her sturdy little legs pushing the push-chair. Suddenly she calls out the only word that she knows: "Ball!" There is no ball to be seen anywhere, or is there? Then I see the round red traffic sign with its white stripe standing out against some green overhanging branches: round and red, just like her own ball at home! On another occasion, the same word refers to a group of children playing with a ball. This plurality of ideas, concentrated in one word, is like the very first budding of a plant which will put out more and more leaves in time. The ideas are already there or, so to speak, "already hanging in the air." The young child grasps relationships between people and things, and acts accordingly. But the art of "capturing" these relationships and ideas in words is learnt only gradually. The ideas seem to remain hovering about the child till the right time comes for them to be put into words. Then greater and greater differentiation between words develops and in time real naming begins. This is the period when the child is always asking: "What is that called? What is that?" And once you have named a thing it often seems as if the child then "knows" what the thing is. The child nods thoughtfully and repeats the name several times, as though tasting the word on the tongue.

Those of us privileged to experience at close quarters how a child learns to talk, know it is like experiencing a part of creation. You can hear the characteristics of your own language coming into being. It is as if you are learning it afresh, but this time consciously. You will notice, too, that every child has its own way of developing language. Consonants cause the greatest difficulty, but how this difficulty is overcome seems to be different for each child. One thing however is certain: just because they do not pronounce the sounds properly, it does not mean that they do not hear them properly. It is not just a matter of being able to imitate the sound exactly. Sometimes it appears that a child hears the sound better than we do.

It is fascinating to follow this process of mastering the language, and if you keep a note of the most striking things, you may come to some interesting discoveries. It is important here, too, to keep your adult knowledge in the background so that you do not deprive the child of finding its own words to describe things. It is too easy to stuff a child full of terms and names. But if you let the child go its own way and experiment with words, you will hear all kinds of original expressions. If I forget to open the window when I am cooking, condensation forms on the glass. We grown-ups say then: "The window is misted over." A little girl who was in the kitchen one day noticed it; it was something new for her and she did not know how to refer to it. But, finding words for what she observed, she exclaimed: "The window has gone away." We know exactly what she was trying to say.

While not correcting children's own word creations, we must be equally careful not to adopt their language ourselves. It is tempting to use childish expressions and mispronunciations as a kind of code-language between us and the child, thinking that the child will then understand us better. Then we are not really doing the child a service. It shows respect both for children and for the language if we use language as purely as possible in their presence.

Nursery rhymes are a wonderful aid to learning to master language, along with counting rhymes like "one, two, buckle my shoe," riddles and nonsense rhymes. As with telling stories later on, it is best of all when we make these up ourselves, as we cannot bring them to life in the same way if we read them out of a book, however vividly we try. Telling your own stories does not come easily for all of us. As soon as our first child was born I began to practise, as my tongue had become unwilling over the years. While I was changing the child's nappy, I would recite the old nursery rhymes aloud. I did not have to feel embarrassed as there was no one listening except the baby. With this practice, I found that recitation became easier and more fluent all the time. The rhymes acquired motion and flow, and by the time the eldest began to talk, I was able to accompany all kinds of situations and actions with familiar rhymes and songs, mostly done in a sort of half-sung rhythm.

It is the same with reciting verses or prayers, although here it is the content rather than the sound which is most important. If we regularly say a verse every evening by a child's bed, then the words eventually flow and take on a life of their own, as if we were an instrument through which the language expresses itself. We begin to feel how it must have been in earlier times when the bards recited their long heroic lays on dark winter nights. There no book was ever needed or looked for.

The layers of meaning in the words of our language are full of insight and wisdom. The word "person" derives from the Latin *per-sonare* ("to sound through"). If we open ourselves to the world of the spirit, something can sound through us, something which we try to grasp in words, capturing an idea or thought. Then as soon as we utter the words, we set something in motion in the world. Whoever has the power of words has an instrument with which to make or break.

Our world of human intercourse is largely

dominated by words. Language, in whatever form, is central to human social life, and something so important can easily be misused. This we notice all too often in everyday speech in which language often degenerates to a throwaway commodity. At the same time we can use language to express the most sublime things. In our relations with others, language has a double edge. We can hurt with words, but we can also console. We can caress or abuse.

Words act creatively and are effective; we can observe the truth of this constantly in life. Through the religious side of our nature, we believe that words are equally effective in the invisible world. If we utter reverently the words of a verse or a prayer, we become aware that the space around us fills. What we also notice is that if our quieter moments are filled with reflection on Christian values, we come to use everyday language with more care. Through using language watchfully and lovingly, we can arrive at a presentiment of the great mystery of him who is named in the first chapter of John's Gospel: "The World–Word." The Word has become man and has dwelt among us.

4

Between measure
and melody

From birth onwards we breathe rhythmically in and out. The first cry is a gasp for air, an urgent demand for life. The new-born child must breathe to bring oxygen into its whole body. Just as everything else in the new-born child is still undeveloped, so breathing is not yet regular. Breathing has to be learnt; the infant child's own rhythm has still to be found.

The child we see lying in the cradle is only a small part of the "person" who is going to incarnate on earth. The greater part is still living beyond time and is invisible around the child. Life without any idea of time, without a conscious beginning or ending, a flow as of water — that is characteristic of early childhood until, about the seventh year, the child is ready for school, and can be asked to appear in the classroom on time.

In those first years it is the mother who gives form

to the child's day. Actually a mother of young children performs a remarkable feat every day: she must constantly maintain the balance between her will to create order and have everything running on time on the one hand, and on the other the desire to take into account the fact that such young children have as yet no idea of time. The mother is the intermediary between time and eternity.

The first weeks after the birth are the most difficult. The child has fallen out of timelessness into the world of time. The mother knows that a day can only be manageable when it is given form. From the very start, she has to establish certain routines: the child has to be washed, fed and have his nappy changed at about the same times. There has to be a time for sleeping and for being awake, a time to play and a time to eat. Every mother experiences that this ordering of time at the beginning is not always straightforward and has its ups and downs, but she knows, too, that the child fares best when there is a regular routine to the day.

In an atmosphere of calm ordered routine, a child can flourish. There is, however, another element necessary for a healthy development, and that element is ourselves. Our attention and our loving gaze are for the child what the sun is for the plant. Through our own warmth and dedication we can impart a rhythm to the orderliness of the day and so create an atmosphere in which the soul of the child can breathe freely.

Even as adults, we notice how breathing is influenced by atmosphere or circumstances. If you run hard you get out of breath. You gasp in fright or joy; you hold your breath in anticipation. Where mistrust, dishonesty and intrigue reign, an atmosphere is created where we cannot breathe and cannot live. We are numbed by it. In surroundings where mutual understanding reigns, openness with regard to each other and open–mindedness with regard to each other's endeavours, there we can breathe and live, grow and work. That does not mean to say that there are no challenges left in life; that would mean standing still and going nowhere. Where there is a true rhythm of life, real movement is taking place, a coming and going between two extremes, sustained by something strong and firm in the middle.

Rhythm is at the heart of music. We often speak of it but it is not easy to say what it is. It is not the same as the *measure* which we might call the skeleton of a piece of music. The metronome cuts music to its measure. But rhythm is not the melody either, the music stream that knows neither end nor beginning. Rhythm is something in between; it holds the middle between measure and melody.

We can find rhythm in the sand–ripples along the shore, in the rings of a tree trunk, in the wonderful crinkles of a cut–through cabbage or in the arrangement of the leaves of a plant round the stem. There is a certain similarity of form, but no one form is exactly like the other nor fits exactly to the other. Each is only an approximation to the pattern with the effect that repetition is never monotonous. Uniformity as we know from mass production is boring and makes us tired. A rhythmical pattern cheers us up and satisfies our feeling for harmony. There is music in it!

The child needs rhythmical order in its life and surroundings and, as it grows a little older, will help the parent to maintain the order already created. Our times of interaction with the growing child will often be centred on these fixed routines: mealtimes and snack times, walk times and washing times, singing and story times. All these create an order that is truly *holy,* in the sense of "healing," healthy for soul and body.

There are three times in the day to which we should pay special attention: getting up, going to bed and mealtimes. These are commonplace events, usually taken for granted, but at the same time in their ordinariness they are a picture of a spiritual reality. Getting up and going to bed are like images of birth and death, a transition from one state of being to another. At meals we take in substances which are transformed through a mysterious process so as to enable our bodies to live and grow.

There is no sense in discussing such thoughts explicitly with young children. With children we must be "doing." What can we do to attach significance to these key points of time?

Words are bearers of thought. The right words spoken with reverence are a worthy accompaniment to special moments. When humankind still stood open to the spiritual world, life was filled with verses and prayers. In the child we can regain this openness which we ourselves have lost.

The moment of awakening is always new. A healthy child has not the least trouble getting up, waking and jumping out of bed as naturally as the sun rises over the earth. Getting up, rising into the proper human position is every day a marvel. In waking we recognize the prototype of all spiritual development. When we gain an insight into a particular problem, we say: "I begin to see light," or "It dawned upon me." We can celebrate the moment of waking with a morning greeting, a song or a verse.

As the day draws to a close, a nurse in a hospital will say to her patient: "We're going to get you ready for the night." Going to sleep is an important moment, especially for sick people. Physical pain is felt more keenly in the quietness and the darkness of night; fear can take on grotesque forms. But the moment of going to sleep is important for us all. How do we go to meet the night? What happens and whom we meet when we sleep we can only surmise; but that something happens is certain, and that there are powerful regenerative forces at work we discover when we wake up next morning refreshed. In order to make it easier for those forces to work on us we must give that moment of transition special attention.

The way we say good night to our children, going briefly over the events of the day, tucking in the blankets more than once and caressing the warm cheek: all this helps to make the child feel secure and go calmly to sleep. On the other side, a higher being takes over the watch. In this atmosphere, we feel strongly the need to carry out a little ritual. This ritual starts to develop from the child's earliest days with us as the coming of the child awakens in us a religious attitude, the original attitude with which we were born, but which has got snowed under during our lives. So now we find to express this rediscovered attitude with the infant child, an evening prayer or a verse is effective. In order to give the spoken word a foundation, we light a candle. The little flame reflected in the eyes of parent and child helps to still the last eddies and impressions of the day, which can now settle down and come to rest. Now we say the verse or the prayer.

When we start this practice, at first the new words

feel unaccustomed on our lips and it is as if we hear a stranger speaking. But after a time we notice to our surprise that the words start to have a life of their own, something flows into them. The strain of having to remember recedes, and the words come by themselves in due course. Then when the light is doused the darkness is no longer forbidding. The child can go peacefully over the threshold to meet its guardian angel.

There is a saying: "One who learns to pray as a child, will know how to bless in old age." For a child, one of the most significant of prayers is the verse or grace before meals. A moment of stillness before we take food gives space to what is truly human and helps us to restrain the desires which belong to our bodies. We create a space for thanking nature, thanking our Creator, thanking those who have brought us our food. Some graces, of course, are too difficult to be understood by a young child, but that does not matter. The child will still absorb the whole mood of the moment, the gesture of the bowed head, and the folded hands.

We have spoken of both verse and prayer. A verse directs our attention to what we see; the prayer directs our attention inward and teaches us to listen. But both are effective when used with patience and constancy. Just as a river carves out its bed by the constant flow of water so prayer can form a conduit for the operation of the spirit. That is true grace.

A mother gave the following account of a conversation with her daughters:

Two days ago I was sitting with the girls at bedtime, saying their verse, as I do every evening. After the words had been spoken, the youngest girl, four years old, suddenly remarked:

"I heard you say 'God'."

The oldest, five years old, asked in a matter of fact way:

"Is it all right to say 'God' there?"

"Yes," I said, "it is all right to say 'God' there." I knew that she was thinking of my strict injunction not to use improper language. Then the oldest added thoughtfully:

"I also heard you say, 'and all that is around me'."

The girls were quiet for a moment.

"Those are the angels," went on the older child.

"No," said her younger sister out of a natural urge to contradict.

"Yes, they are," said the elder emphatically, "all round your bed!"

5

Teaching good behaviour

In a medieval town, plays were acted on festival days in the market place, usually on a dray which was used both as a stage and a vehicle. The spectators were shown two plays: a morality and a farce. The first was to teach people a moral lesson, and the second, earthy and healthy, was to make them laugh. First the ideal, then the caricature of reality. Neither was real, for at that moment only the spectators were real. The morality took place in three regions: heaven, hell and earth. Left and right were more or less firm, but in the middle, on the earth, that is to say, where it all happened, where the drama was played out, there everything was possible.

Education towards being truly human takes into account the dual nature of the human being, the physical and the spiritual nature. Between the physical and the spiritual is a domain where body and spirit interpenetrate. This is the domain of the soul. Here, all during life, the balance must constantly be sought between heaven and hell. It is the region where nothing stands still, where everything is coming into being and where the individual experiences freedom to choose. This remarkable in–between region is the place where religious education can begin.

A farmer does not sow until the field is ploughed and cultivated. Equally, the teacher of religion will be sowing on a hard soil if a child's parents have not worked to keep a certain openness towards religion in the home. As parents, we should teach our children *mores* (that is, good behaviour) as early as possible. The Romans used the word *mores* to refer to customs and usages in their family and society, all that in the course of time had become recognized as decorous behaviour. The *mores* were the unwritten laws of what was "done" and not "done," in contradistinction to the *leges* which were written statutes which came to govern an entire Empire. The *leges,* the work of the *patres,* the fathers, were strict and clear, just as the Roman roads were straight and unswerving, the shortest distance between two points.

Using a paternalistic "straight line" approach, we cannot achieve anything with a young child. The child is still living in a dream consciousness, even though it appears to be wide awake. Children experience this "paternal" element only in so far as their mother carries it in her thoughts. Later when the child goes to school the paternal comes more into its own. At this stage, there are rules to be obeyed. The "ten commandments" rule over the period from seven to fourteen, the period of authority.

If you look at very young children, you will see that they are still living near heaven, so much so that it is as if the sunshine is constantly reflected in them. Long diatribes about what is allowed and not allowed are not called for with the very youngest whose sunny nature stands in such natural relation to God's world. The child lives entirely in imitation, in doing. Therefore we must bring rules and commandments and order to life through our own actions. That is the "motherly" way, which sometimes appears to be a roundabout way, but which often joins up the points better than the shortest way. The "motherly" element appeals to the child, whether it comes from the mother or the father. Both the paternal and the maternal are within us, and both have their moment. Morals should be "taught" in the motherly way, or we might say, morality must emerge from a fundamentally religious atmosphere with young children. Only then will *mores* become true morality.

The word *religio* is sometimes regarded as being derived from the Latin verb meaning "bind again." According to the norms of the Latin language that is not an accurate derivation, but this attempt to explain the origin of the word does say something about its feeling quality. Through religion, we seek to renew our connection to the spiritual world. A child is not able to maintain a natural religious connection to the spiritual world unaided. From the moment when the child is born and makes its first cry, from that moment when the physical connection to his mother is severed, the inner vision of the spiritual world is progressively lost. The moment that the lungs begin to work and the child lives, then from the aspect of heaven a spiritual being has died.

The Ancient Greeks, amongst other cultures, looked on this event as the imprisonment of the immortal kernel of the human being, as an entombment in a coffin with an inexorably descending lid. This entombment means that every individual is a separate being. But the complete process of individualization takes place in a series of steps. At birth the human being becomes a separate physical entity. About the seventh year, the individual's life–forces become self–contained. After another seven years, the soul itself becomes independent and at the age of twenty–one the full individuality of the person is achieved. As we grow up, we become increasingly aware that each of us is a being apart, separate from all other beings, and this awareness increases with age and culminates in death.

The words "sinner" and "sunder" must have originated from the same stem. They are related to each other, two sides of the same reality, and interact upon each other. "Sin" leads to being "sundered," to being outcast from a society. Think of the sin–offering of the Israelites. Every sin, whether it be a crime or an evil thought leads to isolation and sunders us from the stream of life. We experience this every day even though we are not always conscious of it. Sin brings loneliness, a bit of dying, a strangulation from life.

But none of us, not even the best, not even He who was "without sin," can avoid the common sundering. We are not like plants unconsciously living as an integral part of a world of life–forces. We come to earth to learn to know isolation. Isolation is the pre-requisite of our spiritual lives; it is the element which makes it possible for us to be truly human. At the same time it means that we all participate in what is called "original sin."

Even the new–born child partakes of "original sin." This state belongs to being human. As soon as the child is physically born, it immediately enters into a relationship with the powers of destruction, a relationship which belongs to earth existence; and from that moment those powers work in the physical body. From the very first moments of independent existence, the life–bringing oxygen that is breathed in is breathed out again as exhausted air, as poisonous carbon-dioxide, and through the metabolism, refuse-substances are excreted. We find all this is natural, but do not realize that this destruction is also the reflection of original sin anchored in the physical body and that it forms the basis for subsequent personal sins. The young child is not yet capable of personal sin; it can be naughty but never evil. An individual can sin only when old enough to know what they have done and to be aware of their responsibility for their actions and omissions.

We have seen that "sin" has to do with "sundering." In our religious upbringing we should endeavour to counteract this sundering, so that we may heal the connection to the spiritual world which has been broken. That means to say that all religious upbringing must be directed to the healing of original sin. This points to a very high ideal. For it means no less than to invoke healing forces to counteract the increasing possibilities of sinning. In the first years we can lay the foundations for a kind of spiritual health which goes right into the physical. No other period in our lives presents so much opportunity for this. For later life, much depends on the first seven years. The young child calls for the best in us. If we take the child seriously and know that creative forces are active there, we shall feel our responsibility and realize that we are carrying out a priestly task. That sounds very exalted, remote and unattainable. But where raising children is concerned, it is not a matter of what we are already, but what we carry in us as ideal, as our potential. These are forces of the future and they are effective. To know this can be a comfort when things seem not to be turning out right.

When the world was created, God saw that it was good. It is the good world in which the child lives, a wonderful world, truly a world that gives birth to wonders. For a child a day is as long as life itself, so much can happen between sunrise and sunset. Look at the little girl not much older than two. She stands by a flowering plant, a foxglove that has shot up, and looks with utter concentration at a fat bumble–bee that bumbles from one flower cup to the next. The child absorbs into herself what she sees: that dark little insect buzzing its way into an open calix and disappearing completely into it. It looks as if they are created for each other, and perhaps that is the case.

There is not much sense in saddling little children with lectures on God and the world. It is more important that they should enjoy experiences by which they can nourish their innate religiousness: a pause to admire the beauty of a shell on the sea–shore; or a pebble picked up at random, gleaming when it is dropped into a pool of clear water. The moment of revelation can be finding the grey–white fungus which has formed a fairy ring overnight at the foot of a huge beech–tree. It can be catching sight of the flaming colour of a creeper against the shed; or a gleaming chestnut; or the gossamer skeleton of a dried up leaf; or glistening dewdrops on a cobweb. Any of these innumerable wonders in Nature, great or small, can give rise to a feeling of wonder and reverence in the child, and offer an inkling of the sublime greatness of the earth and her Creator.

Reverence is the root of all religiousness. It is difficult to teach; we have to live it in the presence of the children. It shows in the very way we handle things, how we pick them up and set them down. Even as adults, when we start to use our eyes with the same patient attentiveness as a child, then our actions follow suit. This is a path of inner exercise, which the child learns for life through its faultless imitative powers.

From reverence for creation, for Nature, for what men have created, there follows reverence for other people as they are with all their peculiarities. To thank and to give greeting are two concepts linked to reverence, and they become effective only when taught by example. Otherwise they are empty abstract ideas.

They were running along together by the shops, the little girl with her fair curls and the smartly dressed old lady with her grey hair neatly trimmed. The girl was holding the old lady's arm tight and warned her of steps and stones. The old lady was chattering away cheerfully and the merry dark eyes in the birdlike face were looking all around her, but not where she was going.

The old lady had lost her memory years ago and so quite unembarrassed she kept asking the same questions, which the child answered patiently. She greeted passers-by with a friendly nod or a wave of her hand. Then suddenly the little lady stopped in her tracks as a complete stranger passed, looked at the other person and said beaming:

"I don't know you, but I like saying good morning to you."

And then she went on, straight as a ramrod on the little girl's arm.

Anyone who can give a greeting like that at the end of their life is blessed.

6

The dancing year

The year is one mighty rhythmical happening with its high points of greater or lesser moment standing out above our daily lives. The course of time for us is like something moving in waves with crests and troughs, not straight but as it were dancing. So, too, we may well speak of the "dancing" year. The festivals which interrupt our everyday lives bring us again and again into a situation from which we can look back at what lies behind us, and also forward to what lies ahead.

There are all kinds of festivals. First of all there is the birthday, pointing especially to the past. In Holland, the guests all dance round the birthday child and sing in Dutch: "Long shall *she* live in glory" even when the child is a boy! Here the "she" refers to the invisible part of the person, and the song asks that it live in the glory of God just as the angels do. On this one day in the year, a blessing is sung for the child who stands in the middle and sees that the people round about are celebrating his or her existence.

Reminded of their first birthday, then the birthday children are allowed to give away sweet gifts that taste "heavenly." In this way, every birthday reminds us of our heavenly origin, although it is only in later life that we become properly aware, and feel a kind of nostalgia for our heavenly home.

The small high point of every week is Sunday, the festival which accompanies us in the *present.* When our calendar began, the first day of the week was called "the Lord's Day" and so the working week which followed was sanctified in a Christian sense. To sanctify is to make holy, to make whole or healed. Through his everlasting presence, the Lord of the week helps us human beings in our striving to become whole, in our striving for harmony, every day afresh. To become Christian is certainly not a matter for Sundays only.

On the Lord's Day, we create of our own free will a space wherein we can remember the goal of our striving. That is the meaning of Sunday, and therefore it is fitting that we should give the beginning of the day a certain emphasis, so that it becomes clear even to the very smallest child. Perhaps we bake something special; eat differently from usual; lay the table differently from the rest of the week. Perhaps grandparents come to have coffee after church, and in the evening there is an extra long story. As the

If you are interested in
other publications from
Floris Books, please
return this card with your
name and address.

Name _____ Surname _____

Address _____

_____

_____ Postcode _____

☐ Please send me your catalogue once

☐ Please send me your catalogue regularly

☐ Please send me a sample of *The Threshing Floor*, bimonthly journal of
The Christian Community — movement for religious renewal

Postcard

Floris Books
15 Harrison Gardens
EDINBURGH
EH11 1SH
Great Britain

children grow older, the children's Sunday Service helps to strengthen the special character of Sunday. Marking the gateway of Sunday in these small ways, we step out into the working week.

Then there are high points which look more towards the *future,* and these are the festivals of the year. Just as every day meals are feasts for the body, so the Christian festivals of the year are food for the soul. In celebrating these festivals, those in temperate climates are helped by the different ways in which the changing seasons make themselves clearly felt. The Easter festival falls during the unfolding of the plant world in spring. Michaelmas during the dying down of autumn. Christmas comes at the start of winter, and the feast of St John brings in the summer. Out of our religious awareness, we respond to the wheel of Nature, to the cosmic cycle. Each solar equinox and solstice finds its expression in the festival which follows a few days later. In this way we unite ourselves in thought with the seasons, with the life of the earth.

The celebration of festivals is an art which, in our modern world, we no longer understand as well as our predecessors, nor of which we are naturally masters. In former centuries, people still experienced strongly the flow and dance of the year, as witnessed by the tremendous wealth of ancient seasonal rituals and customs. Some of this wealth has been preserved but most of it has vanished, a loss accelerated by the rapid industrialization of society. Urban society has retained only a fraction of the festivals and customs which characterized an agricultural society close to and dependent on the seasons. Festive customs brought colour and variety to life; people were enriched by them, and the awareness of time was strongly and deeply felt.

These days when we can all read and tell the time, the old customs and festivals have lost their significance as a "calendar." Our experience of time has changed considerably. It has become a personal matter: ten minutes for one person is a moment, for another it is an eternity. In celebrating the festivals, however, we have to do with a supra–personal quality. We do not need to warm up the old festivals, but we will discover meanings if we search for the wisdom that lies in them. Brought into our own modern consciousness, the ancient festivals stand in a new light and can be brought to life in a different way.

In every festival of the year, we find three aspects. The first is *remembrance:* the past which we can find in writings and old customs. The Christian festivals in the first half of the year — Christmas to Easter and then Ascension and Whitsun — follow the path of Christ in the man Jesus upon earth. These events stand in the sign of the ascending sun. Two festivals mark the second half of the year: St John and Michaelmas. We are now beneath the descending sun, in a time of ripening and fruit–bearing: what we have received we must now transform into fruit and deed. In this part of the year, the individual seeks his own path towards becoming a Christian, and this is done through thought, through which we unite ourselves with the seasons. This work of thinking consciously about the seasons and the festivals is something new, a task belonging to our times. It is not enough simply to want a "White Christmas" or an Easter full of daffodils and tulips. These events invite us to a deeper spiritual experience. Nature can be a help but we also need to deepen our thoughts. Older children can be made more aware by asking them to think about the forces that must be at work in Nature and about our relationship with those forces: questions such as, what is snow, what forming forces work in it, what is blossom and how do flowers act upon people?

The second element in our preparation for a festival of the year is the *purpose:* why do we do it, what do we want with it, what do we seek to achieve even though perhaps only in the distant future? The celebration of the festival reveals to us its meaning when we realize that it serves a purpose which goes far beyond our personal concerns. By celebrating, by really giving form to the festivals of the year we can gain some idea of the final goal.

The divine forces working in Nature have given much to humankind. Humans respond to this gift by celebrating the holy festivals. In far–off times there was an open connection to the world of life-forces and of the rhythmical processes. As we struggle through the unrhythmical world in which we now live, it is as if the gigantic reservoir of life-forces is starting to be exhausted. But just as it is demonstrable that "dead" water can be made alive again by a rhythmic treatment — by passing it along "flow forms" — so we can see that by following the rhythmic course of the year we strengthen the reservoir of life-forces, not only of our children and ourselves, but of the whole earth.

The festival of Martinmas reminds us that the spiritual world needs our involvement. The young Roman officer, Martinus, met a beggar at the town gateway and gave him half of his big warm military cloak, sacrificing at the same time something of the dignity of his rank. In the night he had a dream in which Christ appeared. He was surrounded by angels and wore round his shoulders that same piece of cloak which Martinus had given freely to the poor man. Then Martinus vowed to dedicate himself to the service of the Risen One and to renounce worldly titles. A long path of spiritual discipline lay before him, but he knew that he would be weaving an imperishable cloak for his Lord. So we too can help to strengthen that element in which Christ lives by celebrating the festivals of the year in thought and deed.

Thinking about the past and looking towards the future, we endeavour as best we can to give form *in the present* to the festivals of the year. This can be a wonderful experience with children. The earnestness of the their preparations shines out in the sunniness of the children. When in all sincerity we seek the meaning of the festival and to the best of our ability give it a form, this can be an important support for religious upbringing and a source of inspiration for other festivals. Children thrive on this. Colour comes to their cheeks and a sparkle to their eyes; joy and expectation tingle through them and they feel more and more at home upon the earth. In baptism, as performed in the Christian Community, the child is touched by earthly substances, receiving the sign of trust in the earth to accompany its journey through life. Through celebrating the festivals of the year we help this beginning, this tender seed, to grow.

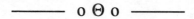

In the celebration of every festival, three ingredients appear, with differing emphasis depending on the occasion. First, a festival is a communal event, and when people come together to celebrate something or to remember something, they partake of a *meal* together. To eat and drink together is deeply rooted in our humanity. A feast is prepared with special care, the table is decorated, ordinary food takes on a special character or appearance: Christmas pudding with its

59

hidden coins (or in some countries, the Three Kings' Cake with the bean hidden in it); hot cross buns; Easter eggs; and so on.

The second ingredient is *flowers*. With their colour and scent, they mirror our soul's need for festival and ceremony. A tribute of flowers expresses reverence, joy or pain.

Light is the third ingredient. On the feast of St John, a bonfire is lit: large, warm and radiant, it blazes up to the stars, just as exuberantly as our hearts follow the ascending sun. At Michaelmas tide and in the deep darkness around Christmas, we turn to candles to impart a living light and reveal the mystery of becoming Christian: the flame devours the candle and so creates light and warmth.

With the aid of these three ingredients — meals, flowers and candles — we give form to the celebration of a festival so that we and our children may find food for body, soul and spirit.

Each festival has its own special characteristic, a certain gesture can be recognized in it. Easter, for example, is an event of death, rebirth and growth — represented by the seed and the egg. Looking for Easter eggs represents the desire to seek, just as the first disciples sought their master on Easter morn; for whoever would become a Christian must learn to seek, patiently and perseveringly. In the Sunday service held for children in the Christian Community the children answer to the priest's question with: "I will seek him."

In a number of countries, stories are told about the Easter Hare who is a symbol of transformation. As a preparation for Easter, during the preceding month we can follow the waxing and waning of the moon with the children, and at story time, we can look for the motif of resurrection which occurs so often in fairy-tales and folk-tales.

As for us grown-ups, deepening our experiencing of the Passion through reading, attending discussions or talks, or even taking part in choral works, will help to make this period the heart of the annual cycle, the spindle round which everything else turns.

Ascension falls in the period when trees are blossoming in orchards and gardens, like a bride's bouquet. In the delicate colours and unearthly beauty and scent of the blossoms, we experience something of heaven.

The special characteristic of Whitsun is harder to see. It is the time of dispersion and the beginning of fruition; the seed of the Word of God is carried out into the world to find a fertile soil.

On the feast of St John, we express sheer joy in life through playing and singing round the blazing fire. The stern message of the Baptist is heard by us adults alone. As a new period begins, it will depend on us whether the new can take root as the seedling breaks through the earth's crust. To sustain the new, courage is necessary, for which we find the inspiration in the festival of Michaelmas. The conquest of the beast in us, physically and morally, is the meaning of the mythical picture of Michael's fight with the dragon.

When autumn storms have passed, we are into the grey days of November, during which the silent language of the dead comes to us more strongly than at other times. This is the opposite side of the cycle to the passion tide of spring. The lives of great individuals — like St Martin and St Nicholas — come to the fore, lives which have become transparent like the windows of a Gothic cathedral. With Advent a new liturgical year begins, a new cycle of Christian festivals. No time is more suitable than this for celebrating with children. Making and baking, carol-singing and acting little plays: there is so much to do that touches directly the world of the child's experience, we grown-ups always feel strongly the intimate warmth of these weeks before Christmas. Through our children it becomes easier for us to believe in the final goal; the overcoming of our inherited loneliness and its consequence, egoism. There is always one force which can do that, and just during Advent we can experience something of it. It is the power of which the Apostle John repeatedly spoke to the congregation in Ephesus. When he had grown very old, his sermons became shorter and in the end he compressed his message into the few simple words: "Children, love one another."

7

Eating on the journey

On the long journey of human evolution, the eating of the apple in paradise was probably the first significant meal. In Genesis, we read:

> And the woman said to the serpent: "We may eat of the fruit of the trees of the garden; but God said, 'You shall not eat of the fruit of the tree which is in the midst of the garden, neither shall you touch it, lest you die'." But the serpent said to the woman: "You will not die. For God knows that when you eat of it your eyes will be opened, and you will be like God, knowing good and evil." So when the woman saw that the tree was good for food, and that it was a delight to the eyes, and that the tree was to be desired to make one wise, she took of its fruit and ate; and she also gave some to her husband, and he ate. Then the eyes of both were opened ...   *(Gen.3:2–7)*

Here it was the woman who sought a deeper connection to the divine through eating of the forbidden fruit. To have understanding, to be able to perceive, to have an insight into the whole of creation like the Godhead itself, all this seemed so desirable for Eve that she risked God's warning of death. Of course, she did not know the meaning of death. But the knowledge of good and evil turned out to be the same as becoming mortal, learning to know death and dying. We have all known moments of insight into our own errors and guilt. These moments hurt; they are a process of dying.

In the biblical description of the creation of the world, the phrase recurs several times: "And God saw that it was good." He could see the good because he also knew what was "not good." Since that critical moment when man and woman ate of the tree in the garden, humankind knows — together with God — the difference between good and evil. This knowledge of ours is expressed by the remarkable word "conscience." Here "con" means "together with" and "science" — *sciens* — means "knowing." However much we know about it, though, evil overcomes us again and again. We become wise through hurt and shame and our knowledge is deepened through painful experience.

After work is done, it is good to rest. As we are told in Genesis 2, God himself rested on the seventh day after the work of creation: "he rested on the seventh day from all his work that he had done." Later the Israelites were instructed through Moses to keep this day of rest as an enduring commandment:

> "Therefore the people of Israel shall keep the sabbath, observing the sabbath throughout their generations, as a perpetual covenant. It is a sign for ever between me and the people of Israel that in six days the Lord made heaven and earth and on the seventh day he rested and was refreshed." *(Exod.31:16–17)*

To this day, Jews celebrate the eve of the sabbath with a meal. Every week on the Friday evening the bond with the Godhead is renewed by eating bread and drinking wine. Thus the end of the working week is marked by a meal.

Over the centuries, this commandment has been the object of so much explanation and commentary that it hardly corresponds any more with the realities of life. For instance, how are we to understand "work"? When Christ walked among us in the person of Jesus, he gave a clear answer to this question through his own word and deed.

Through his example, our holy and healing duty to rest after six days should become illumined from within. We are to rest from forced labour, the work which Adam had to do in the sweat of his brow after the Fall. But what we do of our own free will and out of love for others is the exception that proves the rule.

When the patriarch Abraham dwelled in Ur of the Chaldees, he received the command from the Godhead to go forth to "the land that I will show you." (Gen.12:1) To him was promised: "I shall make of you a great nation and I will bless you." However, the marriage of Abraham to Sarah remained childless for many years. One day three travellers were invited by Abraham to take a meal with him and on that occasion the promise of offspring, countless as the stars, was made for the third time.

From a human point of view, God's plan for the earth hung by a thread as the married couple were already "advanced in age." But with the birth of Isaac, their only son, the eventual coming of the child Jesus would be ensured.

On the occasion of this significant meal, the story tells us: "And he [Abraham] stood by them under a tree while they ate." In the paradise story, too, there was a tree and someone eating. Then it was the human being who severed the connection between God and humankind. Now, with Abraham, it is the Godhead who, in the form of the three men, seeks a new connection with humankind, and does so on the occasion of a meal. Into the human tragedy of the forbidden fruit, there comes a note of hope, and the meal marks the holy moment.

In Greek mythology, we are told how Persephone, the daughter of Demeter, was carried off by Pluto, the ruler of the underworld. Nature withered away because, in her despair, Demeter, the goddess of the earth and all its harvest, forgot her caring task. Finally Zeus, the ruler of the gods, commanded Pluto to let Persephone return to her mother, but only on condition that she had not eaten anything in the underworld. Through Pluto's cunning, though, Persephone had eaten six pips of a pomegranate and so was already united physically with the dark kingdom. Nonetheless a compromise was reached whereby she was allowed to spend half of the year with her mother on the earth.

So for six months each year, Persephone is allowed to see the sunshine. In spring she comes up above the ground as the world of plants shoots and buds, and she disappears again in autumn, when the decaying process sets in with the falling leaves. This myth celebrating the great cycle of the earth and its secrets was nurtured in a temple to Demeter built in Eleusis, where the mysteries were consecrated to the great "earth–mother" who holds the ears of corn in her hand.

In the Gospel of Luke, we read of two disciples on their way to the village of Emmaus. On Good Friday they had experienced the collapse of all their expectations and are now trying to understand events which appear to them so inexplicable. A third person whom they do not immediately recognize joins them. He asks them about their sorrows, and then he begins to expound, quoting the law and the prophets, that the Messiah had to go through suffering in order to reveal the glory of God. When the disciples reach their house, they invite the stranger to have a meal with them. Then, as the Risen One breaks bread, just as he did at the Last Supper, they recognize him and he vanishes from their sight.

These two disciples received an insight into the Christian meaning of suffering, a truth which must be learned on our own journey. At the end of the way stands the "house" of the body completely christianized. That is the goal of our journeying, one that is clearly connected with the mystery of the holy meal.

When we read the various accounts of the Last Supper, we have the feeling that we are approaching the essence of Christianity. In Luke's gospel we find: "And he took bread, and when he had given thanks, he broke it and gave it to them, saying: This is my body which is given for you. Do this in remembrance of me." (Luke 22:19)

In Mark's Gospel is written:

"And he took a cup, and when he had given thanks he gave it to them, and they all drank of it. And he said to them: This is my blood of the covenant, which is poured out for many." (Mark 14:23-4)

Finally in John's Gospel (6:48) we find the great words: "I am the bread of life" following the wonderful feeding of the five thousand, a foretaste of the Last Supper. Here is described how the union with the Christ Being begins with *observation*, receiving by means of the understanding. Then follows *belief*, the going along with movement, the experience of a mighty power. And finally the *taking in* of the immaterial form of Christ in one's own body. What began in the soul and the spirit permeates finally the whole body. That is communion.

> "He who eats my flesh
> and drinks my blood
> has eternal life,
> and I will raise him up
> at the last day."
> *(John 6:54)*

Thus the very centre of the Christian service of worship is marked by a meal in which bread and wine are representative of all the food we eat.

For the young child, every meal-time can be a religious event, a festival celebrated time and time again by the body. What happens when we take in food? In eating and drinking the outer world unites itself with us. We take in substance which is transformed into energy and warmth. We eat something which is visible and it is changed into something invisible. Out of matter arises spiritual substance through a process of being destroyed in us. Surely that is miraculous. It is the most ordinary and natural thing that we know and at the same time we touch here upon the greatest mystery of religious experience. Digestion is a mysterious process which we no longer stop to think about, but about which people in former ages had a deeper knowledge. A meal was at the heart of all the ancient mysteries. In the meal, spirit and matter were united. Eating and drinking were sacramental activities.

There is something else which makes a meal a meaningful event whether we are aware of it or not. When at the end of life, our body is committed to the earth, there too a process of digestion, of consumption, takes place. As the earth is a living organism, does it not seem important how we leave behind our body with all that it has taken in. Should we not then be more careful of our food, not out of egoistic motives, but out of a sense of responsibility for the planet which bears us?

8

Playing is learning

Night falls early in the tropics. We can picture a little girl, about seven years old, lying on her back in the grass looking up at the stars. The night sky arches above her in a great vault. The stars are shining like diamonds on a deep blue garment. Not that she has ever seen diamonds, but she knows them from stories. The longer she looks, the more she feels that she is being lifted up. She lets go of the ground on which she is lying, part of her is left behind and she flies up straight up into the dizzy heights of space.

Then suddenly a star shoots. In the midst of millions of fixed points of light, one star suddenly lets go and sails through the darkness past other stars, and then vanishes, dissolved in the void. A falling star! That means that you can make a wish. And the little girl wishes for a doll with long hair and legs and arms which can move.

Years later when the little girl grew up to be a young woman, she sometimes thought back to that wish. Her mother always said that she was not very fond of dolls when she was a child. What kind of a special wish was that? Were there some stars who recognized her in that meeting in the dark tropical night? She might almost think so, now that she herself has become a mother and sees the eyes of her children shining like stars.

The word "doll" conjures up for many the precious plaything that was inseparably united with them in their childhood years. Amongst all the other toys, children often have one doll of which they are particularly fond. Laura Ingalls Wilder, the author of the *Little House* books, tells how she was made to give her own doll to another child on the orders of her strict mother. The other girl did not seem to appreciate the present very much and some days later when it was raining Laura found her darling doll in a puddle. The doll was taken back with due honour and respect and was cleaned up; and for Laura it was as if she had found her soul again.

The Latin word for "girl" and "doll" is *pupa,* a word that is also used to name a stage in the life of some insects. Once a caterpillar has eaten enough, he goes to "pupate," that is, he winds himself into a cocoon. The pupa looks like a large seed kernel, hard and dry. When the time is ripe, it breaks open and out flies the moth or butterfly.

At first sight, perhaps, there is no obvious connection between a pupa, a girl and a child's doll. But there is young life, growing and developing, in all three. The girl-child sees her own soul-life moving in her doll. All sorrow and joy, and the large or small impressions of the world, are lived out and worked at in the soul which lives in the doll. The child, too, is pupating, so to speak, and the time will come when the person must emerge and fly. There comes the day when the most precious doll is no longer necessary. The soul of the child comes out of the doll and spreads its wings in order to fly and explore the flowers of the world.

Our age has been called "the Age of the Child." Those were prophetic words in many respects. In the western world, our children are dressed in comfortable clothes; writers and artists produce a wealth of picture stories and poems for children; in schools, visual teaching aids have made their official entry and a curriculum more fitting for children has been widely introduced. When the year 1979 was termed "Year of the Child," we were brought round to asking how far the title matched the reality. When we look at the world around us, we are inclined to answer this question negatively. In the conditions created in our own century, it is not easy to make space for children at play. Both parents and teachers have been called

73

upon to use their inventiveness to tackle this problem. By looking at a child properly, we can reawaken the child in ourselves and so find ways to meet the need for play.

For a child, playing is as vital as food. For children always and everywhere, playing is learning. When we watch children at play, we can see them unconsciously working hard at themselves. Playing is an activity which develops with the child through different phases. We might say that playing begins when the child is about forty days old. Then the serious look in the child's eye is interrupted for the first time by a radiant smile. This is when children wake to the world. They discover their hands and after a time they realize that these belong to themselves. With their eyes, they follow the movement of their fingers and start playing with them. That is the beginning of play.

The young child lives much through imitation. So we must make sure that there are little tasks worth imitating. Modern housework revolves around electrical appliances, finished products which offer little scope to the imagination. Disregarding the value of your washing-machine for a moment, it has to be said that a child will get more out of watching an adult wash a few things by hand. Again, dustpan and brush do not go roaring around quite as fast as your vacuum-cleaner, but the action involved is one which can easily be imitated. You can buy ground coffee everywhere, but this offers no hint as to where the coffee comes from or how the grinding is carried out. There are still old-fashioned coffee-grinders to be found, and most supermarkets sell coffee–beans these days.

In her book *The Long Winter,* Laura Ingalls Wilder describes unforgettably how, in order to bake bread for the family, they had to grind wheat grains into flour with the coffee–grinder, their hands stiff with cold.

In the average household, there is still much that is done "by hand," small jobs which can be imitated by children in their play: beating out a mat, sewing and darning, washing up and making the beds, looking after the plants and cooking the meals. Watching and imitating these routine activities is the child's way of becoming conversant with the world.

Play means the same for the child as work does for the grown–up, with this great difference: that the adult works to achieve results and to attain a goal. For a child, the aim of playing lies in the play itself, and seldom if ever in the result. Healthy children play because they want to play, urged on by the warm living stream of their imagination. From the third year onwards, the activity of the child's imagination becomes noticeable, as the wooden block, the chair, a cloth, a box, all become what the child wishes them to become.

A little girl lies on the floor and puts coloured blocks together to make something. She sees her mother coming and chants: "You can't guess what it is that I'm making." Mother suggests something: "a house, a field of tulips, a ..." Her daughter suddenly says emphatically: "I'll guess it myself, shall I? It's a wall! It's a colour–wall!"

In the child's imagination, nothing is fixed and anything can become anything, just whatever you like. Later it is through dressing–up and making "houses" that the child's inventiveness takes form.

Children also need "space" to play in another sense. Playing is of course not utilitarian and before we know it we have disturbed a child at play because it is time to eat or to go shopping or because a visitor has come. Respect for order or rules does not need to clash with respect for the child's play. It requires from us all a little give and take. Playing is a flexible interplay with the world, and we can learn something of this flexibility from our children.

In the garden there is a lumber–shed where old boxes, garden fencing and bits and pieces for the sand–pit are lying about. Under the floor of the shed is a space for logs. In autumn the leaves are blown in, spiders weave their webs, and once a blackbird built its nest there. The shed started life as a climbing frame, a simple raised floor of planks with a railing, a pair of steps at the front and a ladder on one side. Under the planks there was a space to play between the uprights, and near the steps was a little door only big enough for a child to pass. On the wooden floor the children built "houses" with cloths and planks, and clambered about all over the structure. In the hollow under the floor the children could live, baking and frying in all the pots and pans they kept there.

After some years, it was decided to build a house on the platform, and this was done. A little table was made and two benches along the wall. Also a shelf for the pots and pans. Two windows were cut out between the wooden walls, and a door. In front of the windows there were no shutters and the door was usually a hole. The house stood open on three sides, only the back was closed, for there the swing swung past.

It was a nice little house, and yet ... when it was finished it was not played in so much any more. And if they did play the children took cloths and planks to do it up or they built their own little house nearby. When they were bigger, they used the house as a rock-face for climbing, threw a rope over the roof and pulled themselves up like a mountaineer on a mountain face.

Now the ladder is almost a ruin and the ridge of the roof lets in the rain. In time it will no longer be recognizable as a little house, and then it will again be a place where children can build castles in the air.

9

A filled rucksack

It was 1941 and the war with Japan had broken out. The American navy in Pearl Harbour had been attacked and the great powers were advancing against each other. But none of that penetrated to the little girl standing patiently by the rattling sewing-machine. It had been like magic: first a big pair of scissors had cut the long orange curtain into bits, and when she came back to have a look, there lay three neat little rucksacks with strong broad shoulder-straps for her and for her younger brother and sister. The baby could not yet carry anything, and was going to be carried himself.

They had to leave this house, very quickly, and no one knew where to or for how long. The children were told to pack a toy, a book, marbles and a cuddly-doll into their little rucksacks. Mother added some clothes and a toothbrush. Thus a mother and four young children went off to an unknown future, a future that was to last three war-years. And it turned out that each rucksack held a treasure which no one had suspected. In those times of exceptional need, all the ordinary little items came to have a golden gleam of indispensability.

———— o Θ o ————

Some people think that if you tell children fairy-tales and good stories, if you teach them prayers and celebrate the festivals of the year with them, then you are indoctrinating them and they will become inflexible in their outlook; and so they give their children nothing of this. Such an attitude, however, is misguided.

If a child is about to go on an expedition, you fill his rucksack with food. When and how he eats it will depend upon the expedition. Or suppose you give a child a musical instrument and provide music lessons. You hope that something will come of it, but whether anything does come of it you will only see later. In this you have to have trust, for you cannot force the outcome.

A child is not an empty barrel into which you can go on pouring until it is full. Inside something goes on, and often something quite different comes out from what you stuffed in. You teach a child to play an instrument so that he or she can choose later whether to go on with it or not. To make music and to listen to it rightly demands long practice, and that applies just as much to the sphere of religion.

One of the most necessary things that we must pack in the rucksack for life is the fairy–tale, the good old folk–tale with its great wealth of pictures. We cannot be grateful enough to the Brothers Grimm and other collectors for gathering this precious treasure, noted down from the mouths of many story–tellers. Fairy–tales are a great help in the endeavour to keep access open to the spiritual world, or in finding one's way back there later. In listening to fairy–tales, children undergo experiences in feeling and develop qualities of soul.

Out of the many motifs in fairy–tales, I select two for special mention. One is *courage:* a youth goes out into the wide world, loses his way in a dark wood, fights against giants or monsters which threaten him or his princess, and he learns to conquer his fear. The other is *compassion:* a girl is sent away by her wicked stepmother, suffers hunger and cold, learns to live through all sorts of situations and wins over the world through compassion.

The courage to overcome obstacles in order to reach your goal is not the only kind of courage; in our own times it is perhaps more necessary to have the courage to change, to handle new situations, the courage to think the unthinkable. *Com–passion* (meaning "suffering–with") is living out of one's free will with the suffering of another person. It alters your gaze; you look with your heart, and you then see what is really needed by the other person, instead of what *you* think you would like to do for them.

Originally fairy–tales were narratives for adults, not

for children, a tradition that still survives in Eastern lands. The ancient fairy-tales, composed by unknown story-tellers, the motifs of which can be found in all cultures, belong to the spiritual inheritance of mankind. In ancient times, "seers" were initiated into the secrets of the supersensible world. Many seers were blind and could not see the outer world. They received images of the spiritual world and translated them into words. Poets like Homer, who was also reputed to be blind, played their part in this ancient tradition. Popular versions of the old stories and images were spread abroad by poets, singers and story-tellers, so that people were always reminded of the invisible forces working in ourselves and in the world.

The fact that fairy-tales are now told only to children in no way detracts from their spiritual value. Mind you it is also true that a fairy-tale can have a good effect only when the teller is filled with its greatness and truth. If we tell a story only to amuse the children, then we do not penetrate to its deeper meaning; we do the story and the children a disservice. We must be prepared to immerse ourselves in the content of the tale so that we really reflect the images and actions of the story. That is why it is so important to *tell* the story and not to read it. Most of the stories we should tell word for word as they are written, which means spending a little time learning the language of the stories off by heart. There is wisdom in the language which we discover when we observe the pictures from within. It is like the coloured windows of a cathedral: from the outside they look grey and unpatterned, but as soon as we go inside the church the colours come flaming towards us, and the forms become visible in the light shining from without. Something similar happens with a fairy-tale if we take it seriously and try to avoid any form of caricature. Not so seriously of course that we cannot laugh from time to time. There is much humour in the fairy-tales, but it often lies hidden, as it were in between the words. The way we tell the story can release the humour and can make the children laugh. For laughing is healthy and healthy humour is spiritual.

There is a further reason why it is good to tell as many stories as possible without books and pictures while children are still very small. At this early age, words spoken with reverence have the power to evoke images that are alive. However beautiful the picture in a book, it has become fixed, an end-product of someone else's inner picture. Children must have the chance to create their own strong inner pictures of the things they hear about: a king, a princess, a fox, a witch, a girl wearing a red hood. We don't often meet a king nowadays but we can sense that a child knows what a king is when we conjure up the picture by uttering the word "king" and describe how a king rules over a whole kingdom.

In by-gone ages, kings were more common though even then the common people saw them only from afar. The distance was important, because what mattered was not the mortal human being, but the immortal function, expressed in sceptre and orb, sword and robes and above all, of course, the crown. In some early cultures, a person was chosen to be king for his moral qualities. When kingships became hereditary, caricatures of kings often arose, for morality is not inherited. As the development of the child reflects the evolution of mankind, so we can understand that each child carries within the prototype image of "king" and that it is the future of every human being to become a king, ruler over the kingdom which bears the name "Myself."

It once happened that the father and mother of a family were launched into a violent argument by an unfortunate remark. Their five–year–old son was playing in the corner of the room, but he missed nothing. He was immediately upset and started to be sick. Some days later when the episode had blown over, they talked about it, the mother and her little son.

"You know, Daddy was angry really because he was so worried. He was worried and anxious because I was ill again."

To this explanation the child made the comforting comment:

"That's like the story of the seven ravens. The father was worried that the new–born baby girl would die. So

84

he was angry and made a wish and his sons got turned into ravens."

The little boy had recognized the picture and so the problem could be dealt with. Even though his rucksack was not yet filled, the glint of the treasure within was momentarily glimpsed by the mother.

— 10 —

The mystery of the night

Today we pitched our new tent in the garden to check whether everything is in good order, and whether it looks as good as it did in the showroom. The children want to try sleeping in it without delay, but they will have to take turns. The first has just gone off with his sleeping-bag and pyjamas to get ready for the night. He is almost nine years old and insists that he is going to spend the night alone in the tent. He has taken the key of the house with him, and the outside light is left on. I sit and write at the big table in the kitchen and wait. Will he be able to face the confrontation alone with the night?

The twilight is long, as it will soon be the longest day. But at last the shadows creep round the tent, and it grows dark. If you have never slept alone in the midst of Nature, you can never know the special quality of that experience. Or is one person more sensitive to it than another? When the light of day and the tumult die away, a great stillness comes over you in the darkness. Because we are so accustomed to orientate ourselves with our eyes, we begin to feel uncertain when we can no longer see anything. Furthermore everything looks different in the darkness, even in a familiar garden. A child feels that much more strongly than a grown-up who can reassure himself rationally.

At night in the midst of Nature where the sap is flowing, where everything is growing and blooming, where the roots are thrusting into the ground, where everywhere there are powerful forces of growth which by day we can see only in part — in the midst of that primeval process you lie there, a defenceless human child, protected only by a thin sheet, and it is as if the invisible forces are holding a conversation with the forces at work in your own body. You are confronted with the life-forces of creation, with the "Father-Ground of all existence." And the confrontation requires courage, as the young knight Botvid found out in the story of the *Swan Prince.**

At half past eleven, I tidy up my work. I am just going to switch off the light, when suddenly the boy stands in the room.

"I did not dare any more," he said simply.

I get him to go and get his sleeping bag and zip up the tent properly. Then he climbs very happily into his own bed in the stone house with its big protective roof.

---

* "The Swan Prince" by Jeanna Oterdahl. In *The Easter Story Book*, Floris Books, Edinburgh, 1991.

—— o Θ o ——

What is our interaction with night? As adults, we spend a third of the twenty–four hours asleep. That is a large proportion of our lives, and it poses the question why night has such an important part to play. There is a story by Erika Dühnfort* in which she tells how angels have the task of watching over the four directions of the wind and at the same time over the four parts of the day's cycle. To the angel of the North and of the night was said: "Darkness and cold shall be your gifts to the earth and to all that lives on it. You shall be the bringer of refreshing sleep and good dreams. Through your gifts all that has grown tired because of the light and from being long awake shall become strong and fresh again."

That is the first thing we notice about the night: just as it was with the child in the cradle so now it is also with us adults. In sleep regenerating forces are at work, forces which we cannot do without. If we get too little sleep, we can fall ill. Falling asleep when tired and waking refreshed is proof that something has been at work in us. We see how necessary night is, how significant is sleep.

In another sphere, where we have decisions and plans to make, we can gain experiences with night.

* *Vom grössten Bilderbuch der Welt,* Freies Geistesleben, Stuttgart 1986.

There may be a particular problem with which we are wrestling; it appears insoluble and then we say: "I'm going to sleep on it." Next morning when we wake up we may see the solution to the problem staring us in the face. Then we set to work and get to grips with it. Seldom do we pause after receiving this gift of the night, and we do not ask who or what has given us the solution. But if we have to do with children, we ought to ask ourselves the question: who or what do we meet in the night?

In the Grimm's story, *The Gold Children,* two brothers were born on the same day, one of whom goes out into the wide world and has all sorts of adventures while the other remains behind "in his father's house." It is this "heavenly" twin–brother whom we meet every night, our higher I, which over-sees our self–chosen path of life, and by which we are constantly being reminded of our life's goal. The more we are capable of letting go the impressions and emotions of the day before we go to sleep, the more intensively will the meeting come about. That sounds harsh, but the spiritual world has its own laws. In many fairy–tales, we discover this truth about the spiritual world clearly expressed in imaginative language.

We encounter the night, too, in the cycle of the year, in which light alternates with darkness. Winter is the dark night of the year, and at the very darkest moment, when the sun is least visible, we celebrate the great festival of Light.

At the point of deepest darkness, the sun begins to

ascend again and there come the first signs of a new dawning.

The longest day comes in the middle of the year when the sun has reached its highest point. But full summer comes only after that when the sun's path across the sky begins to descend; during summer the days grow shorter and by the end of October we have to admit reluctantly that the night of the year is upon us.

There are periods of decline in life, too, which are hard to accept. Such "dark" periods bring indications that we humans must find new ways of coping. For instance, when our "sun" begins to descend after the middle of life we can postpone the recognition of our decline for a long time. But through accepting everything that is "night" — our declining powers, sickness, physical weakness and frailty — then light comes in that darkness because we have learnt to see what the "night" can give us. In the darkness the appearance of things becomes less important; their inner nature, their true essence, begins to speak, and that is true also of our own inner selves. We are here reminded of the story of the boy who finds a gold coin under his pillow when he wakes every morning. Through entering the darkness of night willingly and with understanding, we shall wake to find gold under our pillow in the morning, a gift from the night.

Many years ago I went to visit a young married couple who had an "unfortunate" child as it was called. The child lay motionless in a box. He just seemed to lie there. At that time of my life I had no idea what to do in such situations. I was inwardly not yet strong enough to perceive calmly, to be able to look at that child and just accept him. Intuitively I could sense that I was here confronted with an aspect of the "darkness" which we have to face in our lives.

Later I came to be sorry that I had not looked more deeply at that child. Years after, quite by chance I read a tiny notice in the paper telling that the child had died. The dates of his birth and his death were the same; he had died on his third birthday. I never met his parents again, but from others I heard that this gravely handicapped child had brought joy and a spirit of tolerance into that family.

11

Death as godfather

Young children look upon death in a very matter of fact way. The child suffers sorrow at the loss, but not because of death itself. In one way or another he knows that death belongs to life as ebb to flood. Children are liable to come out suddenly with unexpected questions about death, such as: "What happens when you die? Are you then very ill?" You try to give a sensible answer, but only when the child has gone out of the door does the significance of the question really hit you.

In the Grimm's folk-tale, *Death as Godfather*, we are told the life of a person and, at the same time, the life-course of every human being. Since Adam and Eve were driven out of paradise, every human being has death as companion on life's journey. The world that we come from does not know death: on earth we come to know death in all its facets. The death of someone whom we knew makes us aware of what that person meant to us. We go over in our mind all the experiences, all the joyful moments, which we had together; but we also review the occasions when we were guilty of unfriendly thoughts and hurtful words. Death gives us insight into the true being of the other person and of ourselves. Surely it is this very insight which we are all seeking on earth?

The truth about oneself, then, can be found in a life with death as godfather. The Grimm's tale lets us see that death appears to us at critical moments, that is to say at moments when we face a choice. But we are not always able to recognize death. Here language comes to help us. At certain times in our lives, we get the feeling of being stuck, a feeling that lies so heavily on us that we say "I've come to a dead end" or "It's a dead loss" and there seems to be no way forward. But once we pass through that point, all sorts of possibilities arise which we had not seen before. Every dead point is a birth–point of something new.

Looked at in this light, the development of the child becomes even more fascinating: after every period of seven years something is finished, something "dies," but at the same time something new is born. In the Grimm's story, the relationship with "Birth" is also shown quite clearly: the child who gets Death as his godfather at his birth receives his christening present on his fourteenth birthday. It turns out to be quite a special gift, the gift of healing, although granted only under strict conditions. Once we gain insight into the laws of life and death we may not break them, for then they will turn against us. Does that not seem familiar as we look at the way we humans treat our planet and

94

make impossible demands on the life of the earth? Surely each one of us receives at birth the gift of healing, the potential to work healing in the world rather than destruction?

There are individuals who, through their very presence, have a healing effect on their surroundings. We should wish that every child becomes such a person. Such people radiate harmony. We have the feeling that with them everything is in balance; though their body may be old and infirm, yet an inner health streams towards us. The word "sound," meaning healthy, is related in its origin to "sunned," being filled with light, with inner warmth. Children who grow up healthily are given protection for life; they can take a knock. Whatever they go through in later life, whatever lies in their destiny, they will be able to grow inwardly through the experience and become wiser.

By the age of fourteen, when Confirmation is due, there is not much left of the natural religiousness of the child. Children who are now shedding their childhood put their parents and teachers severely to the test. They look straight through the grown-ups as if they will say: let us now see if you really are what you say. They do not yet possess enough knowledge to recognize striving, to see the human being in the making. They often see only the caricature, the distorted reflection of the true picture, and then they judge, sharply and quickly. They thrust daggers of words at one another and at us, they can be very destructive and they change their opinions as quickly as they change the colour of their clothes. But what they are seeking is the highest good of all: truth. "What is truth?" It was Pilate who asked this question when he stood before the living Truth himself.

It is not merely for self-protection that we adults now stand back to guard our religious possession from too direct an attack. Young people are more interested in the earth than in heaven. They want to know what the earth has to offer, and this is right for them. They do not yet know that the path goes further, that in the end we must get to know earthly things so well that we can recognize heavenly things in them. Therefore we as parents should practise some restraint, leaving off saying evening prayers when the children protest that they do not wish to carry on in the same old way. We should respect their distaste for Bible texts and pious stories, and cut back on some of the customs surrounding the festivals. It is not a bad thing for adolescents to experience bare prosaicness when they have been given so much in their earlier years.

On reaching puberty, children experience strongly what humanity experienced in the late Middle Ages (fourteenth to fifteenth centuries), namely the stark antithesis of life and death. On gravestones of that period, Death is portrayed very realistically, with the corpse surrounded by pictures of toads, maggots and worms. Through the many images of "the dance of death" in engravings, woodcuts and reliefs, we know how strongly people experienced that every moment might be their last: rattling skeletons followed the individual along life's path, ready to claim their own. People felt deeply that dying was a part of life, and also that death was the great leveller. This is the main reason why the father in the folk-tale chooses Death as the godfather. We all die in poverty: king, beggar, bishop, servant. We all take leave of everything that was dear and familiar: books, ornaments, friends and family, eating and drinking, and finally the body which in spite of everything was so precious to us. Everything that cannot pass over the threshold with us remains behind.

Death makes everything clear and transparent, just as the skeleton of the bare trees becomes visible in winter. When we stand beside a dying person and watch how they go denuded to their stern encounter with death, then we may suddenly see something light up of the true being of that person, and recognize them for what they are in the aura of truth. An encounter with death is also a meeting with truth.

Dying is not reserved to the end of life, as we have already seen. We all know this, especially those who are endeavouring to become Christian. From the earliest days, the essence of Christianity has always been expressed in the words of the martyr: "in Christ we die." We might also say: "Christianity is the art of dying." We must learn to practise dying during our lives in order to become familiar with death, with distance, with bareness.

At no other time of life do we feel so deeply what death means, as we do round our fourteenth year. We often observe in children of that age the urge to soberness in all kinds of areas, an inclination to dying away, sometimes in the extreme and impermissible. With blazing cheeks, a girl stood up in front of her whole class and spoke on her own initiative against smoking and drinking. The confrontation meant dying a little. Where did she get the strength from? Who held her in balance at the edge of the precipice? It must be the One who is called "Comforter in earthly sorrows" in the Confirmation service. Whoever meets him, either in thought or in dreams, keeps the knowledge hidden till later.

The little room was only six paces long and three paces wide. There was a bed, a chair, a work–table and a chest. No more was needed; the girl felt as happy as a nun in her cell. And then there was the window, her opening on the world: the sports–field opposite the house, bounded by the sand–dunes, the wide air with the circling seagulls above and beyond, the sea, invisible, but always present in the salty smell, the sandy earth and the constant blowing wind. In the evening the long shafts of light of the lighthouses swept against the window, short–long–short in strict rotation all night long. She had become used to it, just as she had to the light of the street–lamps in front of the house.

One evening the glass of her window was misted over, as often happened, especially when it grew colder outside. She had left the curtains open and began to draw dreamily on the misty pane. She saw that the shape turned into a cross with a figure on it, the arms stretched along the broad cross–beam. She looked more closely in faint surprise and then she went to pull the curtains.

At that moment she saw it: a shining cross with a shining figure in the middle, close against the pane at the side of the window. She was startled and felt her heart beating when she recognized the dark lines on the misted glass where the light of the street–lamp shone through. At that moment she was so deeply touched that she had to tell someone. She called her aunt, whose house it was, and explained why she had been so startled. Her aunt, now her foster–mother, looked at her in surprise and asked:

"Why did you draw what you drew?"

The girl shrugged her shoulders. She did not know why and she felt the question as a desecration. When she lay in bed later, she felt the bitter taste of not being understood. The vision of the shining cross, however, she carried within her, a secret which was to illuminate her whole life.

12

The angel with
the red drum

There comes a moment in a child's religious development when we as parents and teachers must step back. And if we are fortunate, we may also see how the child's angel steps back.

The boy stood at the top of the stairway with the painting in his hand, turned towards me. I recognized the angel with the red drum, the picture by Fra Angelico that had hung above his bed for so many years. But now he had taken it down from the wall and asked rather uncertainly: "Do I still have to have this above my bed?" I thought for a moment, then suggested that I should keep his guardian angel for him. Noticeably relieved, he came clattering down the stairs and carefully handed the angel over to me.

When I went up to his room later, another picture was hanging above his bed, the pin-up of some star that looked like a gangster with a hat and a dark stubble-beard. I caught sight of the name under it: George Michael. The name of a high angelic being and of St George, his representative on earth, exactly over the place where the "old" angel had hung. Of course it was a "coincidence," one that I knew I could not even begin to communicate to my fifteen-year-old, busy freeing his room from all memories of former times when he was a little boy.

The youngster putting his angel out of the door, is making a gesture that is very significant for his age. He closes a door; the door of his carefree early childhood is shut, and the angel withdraws. Feelings for that warm and familar world of childhood, now lost, are swamped by the desire to go out and explore the unknown country of the grown-up. It is a time of confused feelings and many questions, with occasional moments of great clarity and insight.

One evening I went to say good night to my daughter of thirteen. She now feels herself too big saying a verse together, so I wrote it out for her where it should be near at hand in case she needed it. The overtly religious element now takes a back seat but we still talk for a while, sometimes with the candle lit. As the shadows of evening blur the outlines of everyday things and boundaries become less defined, then we start to chat. And then, sometimes, she finds words to express what she is feeling and experiencing, as if a higher insight is speaking through her and I listen surprised. Once she expressed it so: "I cannot play as I used to. It is as if I stand upon a threshold: sometimes I fall back into the former phase, but more often I am looking to the other side, and then I notice that I understand what they say." The "they" are the grown–ups.

Later she expressed it even more clearly. For a long time she had played with dolls, but once when she had altered her room she took all her precious things to the attic and laid them to sleep in a dark corner. Sometimes she went to have a look at them and then she would play with them for a time. But one day she confessed: "Recently I went up to have a look at Jan (a most beloved doll) in the attic. It was silly but I got annoyed because he didn't answer me any more."

In the difficult but glorious years of growing into adulthood, there is much that is confusing for us parents. It is as if the children are always putting on a different mask and are really looking for their own faces. Physically they are growing out in all directions; they are always wanting to measure their height. They go and stand on the tips of their toes in order to look over our shoulders. It is as if they want to know whether someone is standing behind us. Then it is high time for the parents to step to one side to let them see Who is standing behind them, and in Whose Name they have kept their children company up to now, as best they could.

———— o Θ o ————

A birthday was being celebrated in a neighbour's house. Children were going through the garden in a long line. Two of them made a gateway with their raised arms while the others went under, singing:

> White swans, black swans,
> Who will go with you to Angel-Land?
> The doors of Angel-Land are all locked,
> And every key is broken.
> Can no one make a key for you?
> Can no one open up the door?
> Let them through, let them through,
> The one who's last shall go before.

They sing until one of the passing children is caught under the arch. The one caught under the arch then has to choose between different things: gold or silver, sun or moon, angel or devil. But only the child under the arch is allowed to hear what the choices are, for the guardians of the gateway keep them secret.

Bibliography

Brigitte Barz, *Festivals with Children*, Floris Books, Edinburgh.

Adam Bittleston, *Our Spiritual Companions*, Floris Books, Edinburgh.

Heidi Britz-Crecelius, *Children at Play*, Floris Books, Edinburgh.

Stanley Drake, *The Path to Birth*, Floris Books, Edinburgh.

Erich Gabert, *The Motherly and Fatherly Roles in Education*, Anthroposophic Press, New York.

Michaela Glöckler and Wolfgang Goebel, *A Guide to Child Health*, Floris Books, Edinburgh.

Ingeborg Haller, *How Children Play*, Floris Books, Edinburgh.

Michael Jones, *Prayers and Graces*, Floris Books, Edinburgh.

Friedel Lenz, *Celebrating the Festivals with Children*, Anthroposophic Press, New York.

Dan Lindholm, *Encounters with Angels*, Floris Books, Edinburgh.

Rudolf Meyer, *The Wisdom of Fairy Tales,* Floris Books, Edinburgh.

Julian Sleigh, *Thirteen to Nineteen,* Floris Books, Edinburgh.

Rudolf Steiner, *Prayers for Mothers and Children,* Steiner Press, London.

Ineke Verschuren, *The Christmas Story Book,* Floris Books, Edinburgh.

———, *The Easter Story Book,* Floris Books, Edinburgh.

Children at Play — Preparation for Life

Heidi Britz–Crecelius

Play is more vital for the child's future than many parents realize. Children's fantasies should be allowed free scope, for they are learning through play and the spontaneous creations of their own magical worlds. The more they can be absorbed in their play, the more fully and effectively they later take their place in the world of adults. This book offers many practical suggestions especially for the urban family. Dozens of real children play through the pages of this book making it a delight to read and its conclusions convincing. It is a refreshing and a timely warning for a technological age.

Floris Books

Festivals with Children

Brigitte Barz

Celebrating festivals is an important part of a child's life. Barz describes the nature and character of each Christian festival, its symbols and customs, and gives practical suggestions for celebrating these festivals in the family.

This book is much more than a craft book describing what to do, it awakens an understanding in parents for the festivals and stimulates creativity for a meaningful family festival.

Floris Books